ROYAL COURT

G000152216

Royal Court Theatre presents

FREE OUTGOING

by **Anupama Chandrasekhar**

First performance at Royal Court Theatre, Jerwood Theatre Upstairs,
Sloane Square, London on 8 November 2007.

FREE OUTGOING is presented as part of International Playwrights: A Genesis Project.

Media Partner

FREE OUTGOING

by **Anupama Chandrasekhar**

Santhosh **Ravi Aujla**
Malini **Lolita Chakrabarti**
Sharan **Sacha Dhawan**
Ramesh **Raj Ghatak**
Nirmala **Shelley King**
Kokila/Usha **Manjinder Virk**

Director **Indhu Rubasingham**
Designer **Rosa Maggiora**
Lighting Designer **Mark Jonathan**
Sound Designer **Christopher Shutt**
Assistant Director **Vik Sivalingam**
Casting Director **Amy Ball**
Production Manager **Sue Bird**
Stage Managers **Nafeesah Butt, Susie Jenkins**
Costume Supervisor **Jackie Orton**
Fight Director **Bret Yount**

FREE OUTGOING was first developed during New Writing from India, a week of play development at the Royal Court in collaboration with Tamasha and Rage Productions in Mumbai.

With special thanks to the following for their help with the development of this play: Sudha Bhuchar, British Council, The Charles Wallace India Trust, Kristine Landon-Smith, Carl Miller, Shernaz Patel, Tiffany Watt-Smith.

The Royal Court and Stage Management wish to thank the following for their help with this production: English Touring Theatre, Habitat, Hampstead Theatre, Nokia, Rubicon, Waitrose.

THE COMPANY

Anupama Chandrasekhar (writer)
Anupama is a Chennai based playwright. She attended the Royal Court International Residency on a British Council-Charles Wallace Trust of India fellowship in 2000 and attended Royal Court workshops in Mumbai from 2002–2003.
Plays include: Acid (Writers' Bloc Festival of New Writing, Prithvi Theatre Mumbai); Kabaddi-Kabaddi (International Season/Human Rights Watch International Film Festival 2004); Whiteout (Royal Court 50th reading/BBC World Service); Closer Apart (Chennai); Anytime Anywhere (Bangalore). Awards include: Regional Winner Asia of the Commonwealth Short Story Competition 2006.

Ravi Aujla
Theatre includes: Antony & Cleopatra, Julius Caesar, The Tempest, Midnight's Children (RSC); Hairy Fairys (Brighton Festival); Hack (Jermyn St); Unsuitable Girls (Pilot/Leicester Haymarket); River on Fire (Kali/tour); The Magic Box (Tricycle/tour); The Colour of Justice (National/Tricycle); A Midsummer Night's Dream (tour); Indian Ink (Aldwych); Wicked Year (National); Untouchables (Riverside).
Television includes: Spit Game, Casualty, Doctors, Family Affairs, Peak Practice, The Bill, El Dorado, Casualty, Family Pride, The Specials, Capital City, Shelley, The Bill.
Film includes: The Family Business, Jinnah, London.

Lolita Chakrabarti
Theatre includes: John Gabriel Borkman (Donmar Warehouse); As You Like It (US tour); The Waiting Room, Dragon, A Midsummer Night's Dream (National); Medea (Royal Exchange, Manchester); The School of Night (Chichester Festival Theatre); Antigone, Caste (BAC); Grimm's Tales (Young Vic); Twelfth Night (Salisbury Playhouse); King Lear (Talawa); The Recruiting Officer, Our Country's Good (Swan, Worchester).
Television includes: Extras, Forgiven, Bodies, The Last Detective, Silent Witness, Doctors, Trauma, Holby City, Fortysomething, Unto the Wicked, Medics, Between the Lines, Number Time, A Masculine Ending, A&E, The Bill – as WPC Blake.
Film includes: Venus.
Radio includes: Blacks the Colour, Second Chance, A Broken Nest, Stowaway, Monsoon, Samsara, Sold, Hour of the Star, Shakti.

Sacha Dhawan
Theatre includes: Pretend You Have Big Buildings (Royal Exchange, Manchester); The History Boys (National/international tour/Broadway); The Witches, East is East (Leicester Haymarket); Borstal Boy (Edinburgh Fringe); Skater Boy (Theatre Royal, Stratford East); Lord of the Flies (The Lowry).
Television includes: Perfectly Frank, Weirdsister College, Altogether Now, City Central, The Last Train, Out of Sight.
Film includes: Bradford Riots, The History Boys.

Radio includes: Chocky, Westway, Silver Street, The History Boys, Excluded, The Prospect, Take Away. Awards include: Royal Television Society Award for On-Screen Breakthrough 2007 for Bradford Riots.

Raj Ghatak
Theatre includes: Tales from Firozsha Baag (National Theatre Studio); High Heel Parrotfish (Theatre Royal Stratford East); Bombay Dreams, West Side Story (West End); Hijra (Bush/West Yorkshire Playhouse); My Dad's Corner Shop (Birmingham Rep/tour); Airport 2000 (Greenwich); Bollywood or Bust (Waterman's/tour); East is East (Oldham Coliseum); Don't Look at my Sister Innit, Arrange That Marriage (Bloomsbury/tour); Nagwanti (Tara Arts).
Television includes: Sinchronicity, All About Me, Hard Cash, Out of Sight.
Film Includes: Starter for Ten, Karma Magnet, Dangerous Parking, The Lives of the Saints, Never Say Never Mind, Birthday Girl, Sari and Trainers.

Mark Jonathan (lighting designer)
For the Royal Court: Breathing Corpses, Clubland, Class Enemy, In the Blood.
Other theatre includes: Prometheus Bound (New York); Hobson's Choice, Nicholas Nickleby, Office Suite (Chichester Festival/UK tours); Babes in Arms, The Lady's Not for Burning (Chichester Festival); Honk!, Skylight, Titus Andronicus, The Adventures of the Stoneheads, The Waiting Room (National); The Wizard of Oz (Birmingham Rep/WYP); Uncle Vanya, Galileo, The Norman Conquests, Neville's Island, Jumpers, The Crucible, The Witches (Birmingham Rep); Shadow Mouth, The Clean House (Sheffield Crucible); Paradise Lost (Oxford Stage Co.); Hamlet (Theatre Royal, Northampton); Tejas Verdes (Gate).
Dance includes: Sylvia, The Sleeping Beauty, The Tales of Beatrix Potter, La Sylphide, Napoli Divertissements, Cinderella (Royal Ballet, ROH); The Nutcracker (Northern Ballet) as well as extensive work for BRB including Cyrano and Far From the Madding Crowd and designs at Stuttgart, Berlin and American Ballet Theatre.
Opera includes: Many productions for Los Angeles Opera, Washington Opera, Israeli Opera, Bavarian State Opera, Vlaamse Opera and Opera du Rhin and most recently Il Barbiere di Siviglia for Scottish Opera.
Mark was Head of Lighting at the National 1993–2003 and is currently an Associate at Chichester Festival. (www.markjonathan.com)

Shelley King
For the Royal Court: The Crutch, Mohair, The Burrow, Lalita's Wedding.
Other theatre includes: Man of Mode, Women of Troy, Tartuffe, Little Clay Court (National); Asian Women Talk Back, Calcutta Kosher, River On Fire (Kali Theatre Co.); Paper Thin, Chaos, Bells (Kali Theatre Co./tour); Nathan the Wise (Hampstead); Behzti (Birmingham Rep); Hobson's Choice (Young

Vic); Bombay Dreams (West End); Besharam (Soho/Birmingham Rep); Macbeth (Theatre Unlimited); Orpheus, The Modern Husband, Ion (Actors Touring Co.); A Midsummer Night's Dream, Heer Ranjha, Danton's Death, Troilus and Cressida, Dance Like a Man (Tara Arts); Top Girls (Royal Theatre, Northampton); Damon & Pythias (Globe); Death and the Maiden (Wolsey, Ipswich); The Innocent Mistress (Derby Playhouse); Cloud 9 (Contact).

Television and Film includes: Silent Witness, Banglatown Banquet, The Magister, Code 46, See How They Run, Real Women, A Secret Slave, King of the Ghetto, Casualty, The Bill, Jewel in the Crown, Angels, Tandoori Nights.

Radio includes: The Spiritual Centre, Behind Closed Doors, Westway, The Ramayana, and numerous plays and short stories for Radio 4 and the BBC World Service.

Shelley is Chair of Kali Theatre Company.

Rosa Maggiora (designer)

Theatre includes: The Penelopiad (RSC/National Arts Centre, Ottowa); God is A DJ (Oval House/tour); Waiting for Tamara (Old Vic); Mother Courage (Nottingham Playhouse/tour/Hackney Empire); Waiting for God Knows (Riverside Studios); Starstruck (Tricycle); Everyman (RSC/US tour); A River Sutra (Three Mills Island Studios); Shakuntala (Gate, Notting Hill); Making the Future (Oxford Stage Co./Young Vic); Easter (RSC/Barbican); No Boys Cricket Club, Party Girls (Theatre Royal Stratford East); Happy Days (Citizens, Glasgow).

Opera and Dance includes: Awakening, Another America… (Push Festival, Sadler's Wells).

Indhu Rubasingham (director)

For the Royal Court: Sugar Mummies, Clubland, Lift Off, The Crutch.

Other theatre includes: Pure Gold (Soho); Heartbreak House (Watford); Darfur, Fabulation, Starstruck (Tricycle); The Morris (Liverpool Everyman); Yellowman (Hampstead/Liverpool Everyman); Anna in the Tropics (Hampstead); Romeo and Juliet (Chichester Festival Theatre); The Misanthrope, The Secret Rapture (The Minerva, Chichester); The Waiting Room (National); The Ramayana (National/Birmingham Repertory); Time of Fire, Kaahini (Birmingham Repertory); A River Sutra (Three Mill Island Studios); Shakuntala, Sugar Dollies (Gate); The No Boys' Cricket Club, Party Girls, D'Yer Eat With Yer Fingers?! And D'Yer Eat With Yer Finger?! - The Remix (Theatre Royal Stratford East); A Doll's House (Young Vic Studio); Rhinoceros (UC Davies, California).

As associate director: Bombay Dreams.

Opera includes: Another America (Sadler's Wells).

Christopher Shutt (sound designer)

For the Royal Court: The Arsonists, Serious Money, Road.

Other theatre includes: Warhorse, Philistines,

Chatroom/Citizenship, Happy Days, A Dream Play, Measure for Measure, Mourning Becomes Electra, Humble Boy, Play Without Words, Albert Speer, Not About Nightingales, Machinal (National); Coram Boy (National/Broadway); The Elephant Vanishes, A Minute Too Late, Mnemonic, Street of Crocodiles, Three Lives of Lucie Cabrol, Caucasian Chalk Circle (Complicite); A Disappearing Number (Complicite with Barbican); Strange Poetry (Complicite with LA Philharmonic); Noise of Time (Complicite with Emerson Quartet); All About My Mother (Old Vic); The Bacchae (National Theatre of Scotland); Moon for the Misbegotten (Old Vic/Broadway); Julius Caesar (Barbican); Hecuba, Phaedra (Donmar); The Resistible Rise of Arturo Ui (New York).

Radio includes: A Shropshire Lad, After the Quake.

Awards include: Two New York Drama Desk Awards for Outstanding Sound Design for Not About Nightingales and Mnemonic.

Christopher has been Head of Sound at the Bristol Old Vic, the Royal Court and the National. He is now freelance and is a regular collaborator with Theatre de Complicite.

Vik Sivalingam (assistant director)

As director, theatre includes: When The Lights Went Out (Tara Arts); Broom – Just Say No, Parklife: Achieving Liberty, Head Over Heels (Pulse Festival, Ipswich); Travels To Myself (Teatro Technis); Please Find Attached (King's Head); The Waiting Line (Birmingham Arts Fest); The Hard Way (Soho Studio); Human Rights (Sir John Mills Theatre, Ipswich); Blue/Orange (New Wolsey Studio); Girlfriends (co-directed with Pete Rowe, BAC); Day Trippers (New Wolsey/Theatr Clwyd); Swingin' In Mid- Dream! (Albany).

As assistant director, theatre includes: Rough Crossings (Headlong); The Soldiers' Fortune (Young Vic); The Price, Private Lives, The Tempest, Sugar (New Wolsey); Troilus & Cressida (Guildhall).

Manjinder Virk

For the Royal Court: Workers Writes.

Other theatre includes: Autobiography of a Face (Lyric Hammersmith/tour); Bill Shakespeare's Italian Job (Edinburgh Festival); Come Out Eli! (Recorded Delivery); Unsuitable Girls (Lyric Hammersmith with Pilot Theatre Co.); Wintersun (Leicester Haymarket); A Midsummer Night's Dream (Belgrade Theatre); Millennium Mysteries (Teatro Biuro Podrozy).

Television includes: Britz, Bradford Riots, Ghost Squad, Child of Mine, Green Wing, Ready When You Are Mr McGill, The Bill, Swiss Toni, Doctors, Trial by Jury.

Film includes: The Blue Tower, World of Wrestling, Orange People, Two Minutes, Cross My Heart.

Radio includes: London Europe, Tonight I Write.

THE ENGLISH STAGE COMPANY AT THE ROYAL COURT

'For me the theatre is really a religion or way of life. You must decide what you feel the world is about and what you want to say about it, so that everything in the theatre you work in is saying the same thing ... A theatre must have a recognisable attitude. It will have one, whether you like it or not.'

George Devine, first artistic director of the English Stage Company: notes for an unwritten book.

The Royal Court Theatre in London's Sloane Square has presented some of the most influential plays in modern theatre history. At the turn of the twentieth century, the Royal Court was under the direction of Harley Granville-Barker and staged plays by Ibsen, Galsworthy, Yeats, Maeterlinck and Shaw. In 1956 George Devine became the first Artistic Director of the English Stage Company at the Royal Court. His intention was to create an international theatre of experiment that was devoted to the discovery of the future in playwriting. The production of John Osborne's Look Back in Anger in 1956 ushered in a new generation of playwrights, directors, actors and designers who together established the Court as the first theatre in London that prioritised the work of contemporary playwrights. Among them were Arnold Wesker, Ann Jellicoe, Edward Bond, John Arden, Christopher Hampton and David Storey. New plays were programmed alongside classics, and the company was from its earliest days committed to producing the best new international plays, including those of Ionesco, Genet and Beckett.

In 1969 the Royal Court opened the first second space in a British theatre; the Jerwood Theatre Upstairs has been a site for radical experimentation and has introduced audiences to some of the most influential new voices of the last 40 years, including Wole Soyinka, Caryl Churchill, David Hare, Howard Brenton, Howard Barker, Peter Gill, Martin Crimp, Sam Shepard and Jim Cartwright. Many outstanding young playwrights have established their careers here; among them Joe Penhall, Sarah Kane, Roy Williams, Rebecca Prichard, Mark Ravenhill, Martin McDonagh, Conor McPherson, Simon Stephens and debbie tucker green.

The Royal Court's Artistic Programme is only partially about the work seen on its stages. Many of its resources, and indeed the roots of the organisation, are devoted to the discovery and nurturing of new writers and the development of new plays. The Royal Court is in the business of asking questions about the world we live in and about what a play itself can be. The theatre's aim is to support both new and established writers in exploring new territory.

The Royal Court has a rich and productive infrastructure for the discovery and development of playwrights:

photo: Stephen Cummiiskey

International Programme
Since 1992 the Royal Court has initiated and developed lasting relationships with international playwrights and theatre practitioners. Creative dialogue is ongoing with theatre practitioners from many countries, including Brazil, Cuba, France, Germany, India, Mexico, Nigeria, Palestine, Russia, Spain and Syria. Many of the world's most promising and exciting playwrights have presented their plays on the stages of the Royal Court, among them Marcos Barbosa, Roland Schimmelpfennig, Marius von Mayenburg, Vassily Sigarev, the Presnyakov brothers and David Gieselmann. All of these influential projects are generously supported by the Genesis Foundation and the British Council.

The Young Writers Programme
The Young Writers Programme seeks to open up theatre to the most exciting and diverse range of new voices around today, encouraging and inspiring young writers to use theatre as a means of exploring their world, and helping them to flourish as artists. Week-long intensive playwriting projects for the 13-16 and 16-19 age groups are run during school holidays and each season playwriting groups for the 18-25 age group are led by resident playwriting tutor Leo Butler.

Rough Cuts
The Royal Court's plays have frequently challenged the artistic, social and political orthodoxy of the day, pushing back the boundaries of what is acceptable or possible. That tradition of experiment and provocation is intensified in the Rough Cuts seasons of experimental collaborations between playwrights and other artists, which are presented as raw and immediate works-in-progress in the Jerwood Theatre Upstairs.

The Royal Court's long and successful history of innovation has been built by generations of gifted and imaginative individuals. For information on the many exciting ways you can help support the theatre, please contact the Development Department on 020 7565 5079.

INTERNATIONAL PLAYWRIGHTS AT THE ROYAL COURT

Since 1992 the Royal Court has placed a renewed emphasis on the development of international work and a creative dialogue now exists with theatre practitioners all over the world including Brazil, Cuba, France, Germany, India, Mexico, Nigeria, Palestine, Romania, Russia, Spain and Syria, and with writers from seven countries from the Near East and North Africa region. All of these development projects are supported by either the British Council or the Genesis Foundation.

The Royal Court has produced new International plays through this programme since 1997. Recent work includes On Insomnia and Midnight by Edgar Chías (Mexico), My Name is Rachel Corrie, Amid the Clouds by Amir Reza Koohestani (Iran), Way to Heaven by Juan Mayorga (Spain), At the Table and Almost Nothing by Marcos Barbosa (Brazil), Plasticine, Black Milk and Ladybird by Vassily Sigarev (Russia), Terrorism by the Presnyakov Brothers (Russia), The Ugly One by Marius von Mayenburg (Germany), and Kebab by Gianina Carbunariu (Romania). All of these productions have been supported by the Genesis Foundation.

The Royal Court in India

Since 1996 emerging playwrights from India have been participants in the Royal Court International Residency which takes place for one month in London every summer. Anupama Chandrasekhar took part in this programme in 2000 supported by the Charles Wallace India Trust, who have also supported every subsequent Indian participant.

In January 2001 the Royal Court ran a two week residency workshop for writers from all parts of India organised in collaboration with the British Council and the Artistes Repertory Theatre in Bangalore. The Royal Court team (Elyse Dodgson, Dominic Cooke and April de Angelis) also travelled to Mumbai, Pune and Delhi to investigate expanding the work. Following this, in November 2001, nine of the original playwrights worked with a group of directors on developing their plays with Ramin Gray and Hettie Macdonald. Seven of these plays were shown as part of a festival of new writing in Bangalore in October 2002. Following the success of this project, Phyllida Lloyd and Carl Miller ran a second residency in Mumbai in September/October 2002. The follow-up of this work was led by the same team in September 2003. In April 2004 nine plays were fully produced as part of the first new writing Festival in Mumbai . In June 2005, the Royal Court invited four of the nine writers to work on new plays in London, in collaboration with Tamasha. In March 2006, Phyllida Lloyd and Carl Miller returned to Mumbai to work with a new group of writers from all parts of India in collaboration with

Rage Theatre. Eleven of these plays were produced as part of the second Writers' Bloc Festival in Mumbai during January 2007.

The Genesis Foundation supports the Royal Court's International Playwrights Programme. To find and develop the next generation of professional playwrights, Genesis funds workshops in diverse countries as well as residencies at the Royal Court. The Foundation's involvement extends to productions and rehearsed readings. Genesis helps the Royal Court offer a springboard for young writers to greater public and critical attention. For more information, please visit www.genesisfoundation.org.uk

Free Outgoing is presented as part of International Playwrights, A Genesis Project, produced by the Royal Court's International Department:

Associate Director **Elyse Dodgson**
International Administrator **Chris James**
International Assistant **William Drew**

INTERNATIONAL SEASON

Jerwood Theatre Upstairs

International Playwrights: A Genesis Project

30 November – 21 December
FAMILY PLAYS:
a double bill

THE GOOD FAMILY
by **Joakim Pirinen**
translated by **Gregory Motton**

THE KHOMENKO FAMILY CHRONICLES
by **Natalia Vorozhbit**
translated by **Sasha Dugdale**

PROGRAMME SUPPORTERS

The Royal Court (English Stage Company Ltd) receives its principal funding from Arts Council England, London. It is also supported financially by a wide range of private companies, charitable and public bodies, and earns the remainder of its income from the box office and its own trading activities.

The Genesis Foundation supports the Royal Court's work with International Playwrights.

The Jerwood Charity supports new plays by new playwrights through the Jerwood New Playwrights series.

The Artistic Director's Chair is supported by a lead grant from The Peter Jay Sharp Foundation, contributing to the activities of the Artistic Director's office. Over the past ten years the BBC has supported the Gerald Chapman Fund for directors.

American Friends of the Royal Court are primarily focused on raising funds to enable the theatre to produce new work by emerging American writers. AFRCT has also supported the participation of young artists in the Royal Court's acclaimed International Residency. Contact: 001-212-946-5724.

ROYAL COURT
DEVELOPMENT BOARD
John Ayton
Anthony Burton
Sindy Caplan (Vice-Chair)
Cas Donald
Allie Esiri
AC Farstad
Celeste Fenichel
Emma Marsh
Gavin Neath
Mark Robinson
William Russell (Chair)

PUBLIC FUNDING
Arts Council England,
London
British Council
London Challenge
Royal Borough of
Kensington & Chelsea

CHARITABLE DONATIONS
American Friends of the
Royal Court Theatre
Bulldog Prinsep Theatrical
Fund
Gerald Chapman Fund
Columbia Foundation
The Sidney & Elizabeth
Corob Charitable Trust
Cowley Charitable Trust
The Dorset Foundation
The D'oyly Carte
Charitable Trust
The Ronald Duncan
Literary Foundation
E*TRADE Financial
The Edwin Fox
Foundation
The Foyle Foundation
Francis Finlay
The Garfield Weston
Foundation
Genesis Foundation
Haberdashers' Company
Sheila Hancock
Jerwood Charity
Lloyds TSB Foundation for
England and Wales
Dorothy Loudon
Foundation
Lynn Foundation
John Lyon's Charity

The Magowan Family
Foundation
The Laura Pels
Foundation
The Martin Bowley
Charitable Trust
Paul Hamlyn Foundation
The Peggy Ramsay
Foundation
Quercus Charitable Trust
Rose Foundation
Royal College of
Psychiatrists
The Royal Victoria Hall
Foundation
The Peter Jay Sharp
Foundation
Sobell Foundation
UK Film Council
Wates Foundation

SPONSORS
Arts & Business
BBC
Coutts & Co
Dom Perignon
Kudos Film and Television
Links of London
Pemberton Greenish
Smythson of Bond Street

BUSINESS BENEFACTORS &
MEMBERS
Grey London
Hugo Boss
Lazard
Merrill Lynch
Tiffany & Co.
Vanity Fair

PRODUCTION SYNDICATE
Anonymous
Dianne & Michael Bienes
Ms Kay Ellen Consolver
Mrs Philip Donald
Daniel & Joanna Friel
John Garfield
Peter & Edna Goldstein
Miles Morland
Daisy Prince
William & Hilary Russell
Jon & NoraLee Sedmak
Ian & Carol Sellars

INDIVIDUAL MEMBERS
Patrons
Anonymous
Katie Bradford
Simon & Karen Day
Cas Donald
Tom & Simone Fenton
Tim Fosberry
John Garfield
Nick Gould
Sue & Don Guiney
Richard & Marcia Grand
Charles & Elizabeth
Handy
Jan Harris
Jack & Linda Keenan
Pawel & Sarah Kisielewski
Kathryn Ludlow
Deborah & Stephen
Marquardt
Duncan Matthews QC
Miles Morland
Jill & Paul Ruddock
William & Hilary Russell
Ian & Carol Sellars
Jan & Michael Topham

Benefactors
Anonymous
Martha Allfrey
Amanda Attard-Manché
Jane Attias
Varian Ayers & Gary
Knisely
John & Anoushka Ayton
Mr & Mrs Gavin Casey
Sindy & Jonathan Caplan
Jeremy Conway & Nicola
Van Gelder
Robyn Durie
Hugo Eddis
Joachim Fleury
Beverley Gee
Lydia & Manfred Gorvy
Claire Guinness
Sam & Caroline Haubold
The Hon. Mrs George Iliffe
Nicholas Josefowitz
David Kaskell &
Christopher Teano
Peter & Maria Kellner
Colette & Peter Levy

Larry & Peggy Levy
Emma Marsh
Barbara Minto
Pat Morton
Elaine Potter
Kadee Robbins
Mark Robinson
Lois Sieff OBE
Brian D Smith
Sue Stapely
Carl & Martha Tack
Amanda Vail

Associates
Anonymous
Cynthia Corbett
Andrew Cryer
Shantelle David
Kim Dunn
Celeste Fenichel
Charlotte & Nick Fraser
Gillian Frumkin
Julia Fuller
Sara Galbraith &
Robert Ham
Linda Grosse
David Lanch
Lady Lever
Mr Watcyn Lewis
Annie Macdonald
David Marks
Robert & Nicola
McFarland
Gavin & Ann Neath
Janet & Michael Orr
Pauline Pinder
William Poeton CBE &
Barbara Poeton
Jenny Sheridan
Gail Steele
Nick Steidl
Silke Ziehl

New book
out now!

THE ROYAL COURT THEATRE INSIDE OUT

For the first time the Royal Court reveals the extraordinary behind-the-scenes story of the world's most renowned new writing theatre.

Spanning five decades, it includes exclusive interviews and personal anecdotes with the people who shaped the theatre and its plays, and made it what it is today.

Available from the bookshop now.

£20

Published by Oberon Books

020 7565 5000
www.royalcourttheatre.com

FREE OUTGOING

Anupama Chandrasekhar

Characters

MALINI, *thirty-eight, Deepa and Sharan's mother, single, accountant and part-time saleswoman for metal polish*

SHARAN, *sixteen, Deepa's older brother*

RAMESH, *forty-seven, accountant, Malini's colleague*

NIRMALA, *fifties, school principal*

SANTHOSH, *forties, businessman*

KOKILA, *thirties, Malini's neighbour*

USHA, *journalist*

Setting

The action takes place in MALINI's *flat in Chennai, India.*

Note

SMS: short messaging servive (text messages)
MMS: multimedia messaging service (multimedia messages)

A forward slash (/) in the text indicates the point of interruption by the next speaker.

This text went to press before the end of rehearsals and so may differ slightly from the play as performed.

Scene One

Wednesday. Around 6 pm. RAMESH *and* MALINI.

RAMESH. I have a stainless-steel bowl at home.

MALINI. No steel. No metal. Metal reacts. Only ceramic. We add two cups of water.

RAMESH. And water should be Bisleri?

MALINI. *Adhellaam vendaam.* [That's not necessary.] Tap water will do. What's important is proportion. See the mark here? Two cups to two spoons of Super Sparkler.

RAMESH. No metal spoons also?

MALINI. Right! We will provide you ceramic bowl, measuring cups and spoons. All free.

RAMESH. It is bubbling.

MALINI. We wait for the solution to settle. (*Pause.*) We need old blackened silver. Mine are all polished. Advantage of having a permanent supply of Super Sparkler!

RAMESH. *Andhuh* [Those] prize cups?

MALINI. Deepa's? Oh, the big one is very recent – for an essay competition. They're not silver. Schools-*laan* [and all] don't award real silver these days.

RAMESH. What about your *metti* [toe ring]?

MALINI. It is looking very dull, *le?*

MALINI *tries to remove the toe ring.*

RAMESH (*re: toe ring*). It misled me for a very long time. I thought you had a husband hidden away.

MALINI. It's stuck to my skin now.

RAMESH. I have a silver chain.

RAMESH *removes the chain from around his neck and gives it to her.*

3

MALINI. Good! We put it in the solution and wait.

MALINI puts it in the bowl. Pause. MALINI catches RAMESH looking at her.

RAMESH. I – I like reviewing your ledgers. Tidy, numbers tally and everything is up-to-date. You are a thorough professional.

MALINI. Thanks.

Pause.

RAMESH. Cost accountant. Mother. Then this. Super Sparkler superwoman, I say!

MALINI. Well. The solution is reacting with silver now! It is cleaning years of dirt and oxidation.

MALINI looks into the bowl.

RAMESH. You have an interesting frown.

SHARAN enters. He's in a state.

MALINI. Sharan! I've been trying to reach you all evening.

SHARAN storms towards Deepa's room.

She's not home yet. Special class – your shoes! Don't bring dirt inside! Sharan!

SHARAN opens Deepa's door and looks in.

I told you she isn't here. Now will you remove your shoes?

SHARAN retreats, begins to remove his shoes, socks.

Ennuh aachu? [What happened?] You look –

SHARAN mumbles.

Sharan? *Ennuh da?* What's –

SHARAN. Will you freaking leave me alone!

MALINI. Mind your language! I pay the bills here. Will you please leave your angst at the doorstep along with your footwear?

Pause.

Where were you all evening?

SHARAN. Sports. I had hockey – hockey trials. Just . . . playing.

MALINI. And you couldn't have told me you'd be late?

SHARAN *doesn't respond*.

(*To* RAMESH.) These boys! I tell you! *Eppo paaru* [all the time], they're busy sending SMSs left, right and centre, but they can't find time to send one to their mother. Or call, though their outgoing calls to me are all free.

RAMESH. This is . . . ?

MALINI. Sharan, my oldest. He's in the twelfth. Deepa is a year younger. She has her heart set on medicine. I think if she puts her mind to it, she can get in on merit. And she sends me SMSs to let me know where she is.

RAMESH (*to* SHARAN). And what do you plan to do?

SHARAN *puts his footwear on the shelf with some aggression*.

MALINI. Engineering. Depends on his marks. (*Re: the chain*.) Can you see? Already the blackness is disappearing. In a few more minutes your chain will be sparkling new!

They look into the bowl.

What?

SHARAN. Nothing.

RAMESH *clears his throat*.

MALINI. Oh, didn't I introduce you? This is Ramesh, my colleague.

RAMESH. Friend. Hello. I thought you had little-little children. I did not / expect –

MALINI. Little? Not any more.

RAMESH. But you look so young!

MALINI *laughs*.

SHARAN (*a bit sharply*). She's thirty-eight.

MALINI (*snaps*). I thought you and Jeevan would be studying here when I got back from office. Well? Is he coming by later?

SHARAN. No.

MALINI. Why not?

SHARAN. He has to – mind his dad's shop.

RAMESH. Can I have a glass of water?

MALINI. There we are! We are done. (*She wipes the chain dry*.) Isn't it bright and shiny now?

RAMESH. Very nice.

MALINI. Look at it against the sunlight. Go on.

RAMESH *goes to the window.*

(*To* SHARAN.) *Iru!* [Wait!]

SHARAN. What?

MALINI (*to* RAMESH). Isn't it sparkling like new?

RAMESH. Can I use it on gold?

MALINI. I have another product called Super Gold. Tell you what? I'll give it to you free with Super Sparkler.

RAMESH. 350 you said . . .

MALINI. I'll give it for 300. But not less than that. I'm doing away with my profit only because you are my colleague –

RAMESH. Friend.

MALINI. Friend. I'll get a fresh packet. (*Hisses to* SHARAN.) Come.

MALINI *moves to the stack of Super Sparklers.* SHARAN *joins her. The following conversation between* SHARAN *and* MALINI *takes place out of earshot of* RAMESH.

I told you not to use up all the water this morning.

SHARAN. It's not my fault.

MALINI. It never is.

SHARAN. She used it all up, okay?

MALINI. All I asked of you was to keep aside a little before you had your bath. If you can't handle a basic chore you should let me know. I'll make some other arrangement. You are not a child any more. Look what you made me do. We are nearly out of Bisleri now.

Temple bell rings.

RAMESH. Six-*aa* already? How time flies when one is enjoying oneself!

MALINI. Do you want to buy some packets for your friends?

RAMESH. Packets? I –

MALINI. They'll love it.

RAMESH. I know, but –

MALINI. How many? Three? Four?

RAMESH. No, I think one –

MALINI. Two? Wonderful! You are a generous soul.

Pause.

RAMESH. Yes. Malini. Um. Water, please?

MALINI (*laughs*). Oh, silly me, haven't I brought you a glass yet?

MALINI *hands* RAMESH *the packets.*

There you are. Super Sparkler. That's 700 rupees but you need to pay only 600.

Landline rings. SHARAN *quickly picks it up.*

SHARAN. Where the hell are you?

MALINI. *Deepaavaa?*

SHARAN. I don't know. They hung up.

MALINI*'s cellphone beeps.* SHARAN *tries to find it but* MALINI *has already opened her handbag. She answers it.*

MALINI (*to* RAMESH). *Oru* [One] second, unh?

RAMESH. No problem.

MALINI (*into cellphone*). Is your class over? . . . Then come home straight. It's getting dark.

RAMESH *picks up the Bisleri bottle used for the demo. He looks to see what* MALINI *and* SHARAN *are up to.*

Is your cycle repaired yet? . . . How much longer is it going to take? . . . You said it was only a small puncture . . . *Sharan-uh anupattumaa?* [Shall I send Sharan?]

SHARAN. No! Let her come back by herself.

MALINI. She's your sister.

SHARAN. That's not my fault!

RAMESH *takes a few gulps from the bottle.* MALINI *catches* RAMESH *drinking.*

RAMESH. I – I hope you don't mind.

MALINI. Oh. (*Pause.*) No, no, it's quite – all right.

RAMESH *finishes the bottle.*

(*Into cellphone.*) I can't follow you if you speak so fast. Do you want to be picked up or not? . . . No, he's not busy.

SHARAN. I'm not her keeper.

MALINI *glares at* SHARAN.

MALINI. If you're sure . . . Fine, take an auto . . . Tell the driver to take the main road.

Ask the driver to drop you right in front of the gate . . . take down the licence-plate number and SMS it to me. *Seriyaa?* [Okay?]

MALINI *switches off the cellphone and puts it back in her bag.*

SHARAN (*hesitantly*). Ma.

RAMESH. The heat is terrible.

MALINI. What? Oh. Yes, yes. Summer's getting longer and longer these days.

Water lorry hoots.

RAMESH. What about Super Gold?

MALINI. Oh, didn't I give it? So sorry.

Water lorry hoots again. MALINI *goes back to the stack.*

Are you or aren't you going to get us water before the lorry leaves?

SHARAN. It's not my turn.

MALINI. She can't get here in time. When will you learn to be responsible?

SHARAN. Why don't you tell your darling daughter that?

MALINI (*to* RAMESH). Be with you in a minute!

RAMESH. I can wait. I don't mind. This is a place where I can happily wait.

> SHARAN *stalks into the kitchen.*

MALINI. Here they are. Your own personal jeweller.

> MALINI *gives* RAMESH *two small packets of Super Gold.* RAMESH *takes out his wallet and pulls out 600 rupees.* SHARAN *comes out with plastic buckets.* MALINI *has steered* RAMESH *so his back is turned to* SHARAN *and the exit.*

Would you – would you know anyone else who would be interested in Super Sparkler?

RAMESH. Well. My sister-in-law may be.

> SHARAN *sneaks past the adults. He exits.*

MALINI. That would be wonderful!

RAMESH. Yes. Let me, let me find out and get back to you. And next time I can introduce myself properly to both your children before they become world-famous doctors and engineers and charge me for coming to see them.

> MALINI *laughs. She takes the money.*

Scene Two

Thursday. 11 am. MALINI *and* NIRMALA. NIRMALA *is clutching a plastic shopping bag.*

MALINI. Is she all right? I left my quarterly report midway and rushed home immediately. You sounded very grim over the phone.

NIRMALA. She's fine.

MALINI. Her hands were very cold. I hope she's not coming down with something. Her exams are too close.

NIRMALA. Her health is not the reason why I brought her home.

MALINI. Oh. Shall I get you something, tea, coffee – I remember you loved my masala tea at the PTA last month. I can –

NIRMALA. Please sit down, Mrs Haridas. This is not a social visit. (*Pause.*) It's always difficult to talk to parents about such things. One would think I had enough training and experience.

MALINI. It can't be her studies. She, she topped the class in the last exams – nearly topped – she came second.

NIRMALA. She is a bright child. We had high hopes for her.

MALINI. Do you know she won the national essay competition last month? She came third. Out of 4,500 children. That puts her among the top one per cent of children her age. With Sharan, you have to, to push him to do something, but she's self-motivated.

NIRMALA *gives* MALINI *the plastic bag*.

What's all this? (*She looks inside the bag*.) Test notebooks, practical records . . . why are you giving me this?

NIRMALA. Mrs Haridas, have you noticed anything different or strange in Deepa's behaviour of late?

MALINI. No, Madam. She's always been an affectionate child. (*Pause.*) Well. She and Sharan did have a huge row yesterday. Over a very silly issue. You see, it was Deepa's turn to fill up water but I made Sharan do it instead – *Appa!* [My!] The two can bicker! But it's not unusual.

NIRMALA. I doubt that's the reason why they fought. Do you know where she was at 7 pm on Tuesday?

MALINI. She was . . . let me see, at the cycle shop. Yes, her cycle had a puncture. She hitched a ride home with a friend.

NIRMALA. Who?

MALINI. Shweta. She's in Deepa's class – of course you'll know that. (*Pause.*) See? Deepa's got twenty-four out of twenty-five in her botany test last month.

NIRMALA. I don't think it was Shweta who dropped your daughter home. How do I say this? Your daughter was not in the cycle shop at 7 pm. She was in the English room. With a boy. Do you know Jeevan Kumar? He is in Sharan's class.

MALINI. Jeevan? He comes over all the time. (*Pause.*) Ah, I see. It's easy to mistake friendship as, as something else. The three of them are great friends.

NIRMALA. There's no mistake, Mrs Haridas. Your daughter is – how shall I put it? – she's been intimate with Jeevan.

Pause.

MALINI. Intimate as in . . . ?

NIRMALA. Yes.

MALINI. They . . . touched?

NIRMALA. Well, yes . . . but more.

Pause.

MALINI. You really have to be clear about what you're accusing my daughter of. (*Pause.*) Did they kiss?

NIRMALA. Do you want me to spell it out – they did everything, Mrs Haridas. She went all the way. Please understand.

MALINI. Deepa?

NIRMALA. Yes.

MALINI. Are you saying she had . . . ?

NIRMALA. Yes.

MALINI (*laughs*). My Deepa?

NIRMALA. Yes.

MALINI. *Che che*. Not my daughter, Madam. There's absolutely no chance of that ever happening! For a moment you had me worried. (*Laughs.*) Deepa and Jeevan!

NIRMALA. Miss Kala saw them together.

MALINI. Then she's mistaken. You're talking about my child here! You know very well, Deepa is not like that.

NIRMALA. At one time, I used to think that too.

MALINI. They're all good friends, Madam. Both my children and Jeevan. It is possible the two were just exchanging CDs – They do it all the time. You know how things get blown out of proportion here!

NIRMALA. Miss Kala saw much more than that.

MALINI. She saw someone else. Look – You yourself said it was seven in the evening. It must have been dark then. The rooms are not all that well lit in the school – I'm not complaining – but you see how easy it is to slip up.

NIRMALA. I asked Deepa this morning in my office if she had (*Low tone:*) sex (*Normal tone:*) with Jeevan. She denied it initially.

MALINI. I told you –

NIRMALA. Then when I probed, she admitted.

MALINI. No, no. That's not possible. (*Pause.*) She's a child. This is all too much for her. She must have been so frightened by, by all these stupid, senseless accusations, she must have confessed to something she never did. Like all those torture victims. Madam, I'm truly shocked at your underhand tactics. No wonder the child seemed so . . . shaken up.

NIRMALA. I did not have to resort to coercion, if that's what you're implying. I didn't have to because Deepa was very frank about what she did. No qualms about it at all. As if I asked her if she'd had lunch. (*Gentler.*) I know, this arrogance is not like her at all. I presume she was a very scared child when she owned up.

MALINI. Honestly, she doesn't even know what is involved in the act. She made it all up. She has a very active imagination and, and –

NIRMALA. Deepa wasn't making it all up. Jeevan has confessed too.

Silence.

MALINI. What exactly did he confess to?

NIRMALA. The . . . act.

MALINI. Deepa! *Vaa ingey!* [Come here!]

NIRMALA. No, don't.

MALINI. We can set this straight right here. She'll tell you she's innocent.

NIRMALA. No! I've heard enough from her. I don't want to see her again today. (*Pause.*) Mrs Haridas. We've suspended her – both her and Jeevan – for one month.

Silence.

MALINI. Suspended?

NIRMALA. Yes. I'm sorry.

MALINI. Look – she, she's lying about it for some reason. Punish her for lying. Punish her other ways. Not suspension, Madam. It is too harsh.

NIRMALA. I'm as shocked as you are. I would never have expected this of Deepa. Jeevan, yes. But not Deepa.

MALINI. What will people say? They'll think she's that sort of a girl. And you know she isn't.

Pause.

NIRMALA. Isn't there any man in your family who might stay with you for some time? Brothers? Your father or father-in-law?

MALINI (*beat*). No. Not any more.

NIRMALA (*sighing*). That's very unfortunate. Mrs Haridas, I'm sorry but I can't help you.

MALINI. Her entrances, scholarships, everything will be ruined. Madam, you are in the business of giving children their future.

NIRMALA. You have to understand my position as well. I have a duty to maintain morality in this school. In the end, I am answerable to society, to other parents.

MALINI. I am a parent too. I pay the fees too. You must give my child a fair hearing.

NIRMALA. Are you teaching me how to be a principal now?

MALINI. No, no, Madam. Please listen. You know, I've stood by you, when you wanted to expand the school premises. I supported your decisions at all times at the PTA meetings. You once called me a model parent –

NIRMALA. That was when I thought you had a model child. (*Pause.*) I probably would have given her some other punishment. Unfortunately, other children know about it now. Some boys were caught teasing Deepa this morning. News like this certainly travels fast, doesn't it? I can't look the other way now and allow her to go unpunished. (*Pause.*) I care about her future too. Be thankful I'm only suspending her for a short while.

13

MALINI. I can get the parents together. They will have something to say when they find out you've penalised a student wrongly. I will have to take legal action. I don't want to do that. But if I have to, I will.

NIRMALA. The sooner you believe it, the better it is for all of us.

MALINI. Madam –

NIRMALA. There are some implications to be considered. Because of a foolish and impulsive act, your daughter could have got pregnant – let me finish – if she is pregnant, what do you propose to do about it? This is a matter that you have to decide for her, as her mother, because she's too young to decide on her own.

MALINI *shakes her head, 'no, no, no, no'.*

In my times, a girl like that was called a slut. Strangely, the boys who were teasing her – they used the same word. Times haven't changed all that much, have they? You have to tread carefully now. Labels like that tend to stick for life. I suspect you'll need the month to sort it all out.

NIRMALA *gets up to leave.*

I think she also needs the time to reflect on what she did. After you've talked to her, I'd suggest you go through her bag. Perhaps you might find something that can give you the answers you are looking for – I don't know.

MALINI. All I'm asking is a chance to prove her innocence. Please give me time. Give me a week to prove it to you. If I can't, you can punish her all you want. Please don't take any action on her now.

NIRMALA (*considering* MALINI). You don't know your child all that well, do you?

Scene Three

Thursday. 4 pm. MALINI *and* SANTHOSH.

MALINI. Do you know how many cups of coffee I've made for Jeevan while he studied for his exams here? I welcomed him into my home with open arms. I treated him better than my own son.

SANTHOSH. I'm really very sorry. I've confiscated his phone. This was the first punishment I could think of.

MALINI. And that will do, do you think? How will that set matters right?

SANTHOSH. It's a start. (*Pause*.) I'm glad you called. But I would have come even if you hadn't. (*Pause*.) This is an awkward situation. But we can firefight it together, it's a question of how we galvanise our forces, how we strategise –

MALINI. This is not a business. My daughter's future is at stake here. Your son violated my daughter. What are you going to do about it?

Pause.

SANTHOSH. What are you talking about?

MALINI. She's sitting shell-shocked in her room because of your son. Jeevan ruined her. On top of that, she's been suspended – for no fault of hers. How is she going to heal?

SANTHOSH. This is, this is — She participated in the act. They were equal participants.

MALINI. Is that what he said? Did he tell you he gave my daughter a bottle of Fanta before he suggested that they go to the English room? He gave her a Fanta. (*Pause*.) Do you know what that means? He put something in that Fanta.

SANTHOSH. Like what? A drug? My son did not drug your daughter! He didn't need to. She was willing enough –

MALINI. There are new-new drugs these days for this sort of an activity, drugs that can make people do things they don't want to.

SANTHOSH. Look, the drugs, you're talking premeditation here. What they did was not planned. Jeevan didn't expect it to go this far. He says he only took her to the English room for a, for a kiss —

MALINI. Oh please!

SANTHOSH. Maybe a little more than a kiss. Whatever it was, they were too young and it got out of hand. Blame it on youth, curiosity, heat of the moment. (*Pause*.) Let me speak to your daughter.

MALINI. No. There is no need for that. She's been through enough already.

15

SANTHOSH. Before you accuse my son, I'd suggest you ask your daughter again. I'm sure she has something else to say.

MALINI. What can she say? She was not in full control of her faculties. Jeevan should take full responsibility. He should confess to the principal. Or I can make it very difficult for you. I can go to the police. I can file a complaint of rape with the police.

SANTHOSH. Oh, will you stop going on and on. I understand your anger, to an extent. But the cellphone tells a completely different story, don't you think?

Pause.

MALINI. What cellphone?

SANTHOSH. The cellphone, um, thing.

MALINI. What thing? (*Pause.*) What thing?

SANTHOSH *gives her a cellphone.* MALINI *takes it. The film starts, she looks at it, she is shocked.*

What is the meaning of this?

SANTHOSH. She didn't tell you, did she?

MALINI. What sort of a woman do you take me for?

SANTHOSH. Please, watch it.

MALINI. Go away, get away, first your son, now you, dirty, filthy –

SANTHOSH. Watch it fully. You'll understand. Please. Let me –

SANTHOSH *moves to take his cellphone from her.* MALINI *slaps him.*

MALINI. *Porikki* rascal! [Lech!] Get away from me, get away.

SANTHOSH. I'm sorry – I'm only restarting it.

MALINI. That won't be necessary. Take it.

When SANTHOSH *doesn't move, she drops the cellphone on the sofa like a red-hot coal.*

Take it, take it, bastard pervert!

SANTHOSH. It's important that you watch the film. Please.

SANTHOSH *takes the cellphone, he restarts the film and hands it to* MALINI.

16

Watch the bloody film, all right?

She takes it. She watches. She moves away from SANTHOSH. *She finds herself near the window. She jerks away from the window.*

I have put it on mute. There's audio as well.

She watches with her back turned to SANTHOSH. *Silence. She can't watch it any more. Long silence. She finally turns to* SANTHOSH. *She's unsure, trembling.*

MALINI. W-what are you trying to say?

SANTHOSH. The clothes that, that she, before she – the cream shirt, it's the school uniform.

MALINI. Are you implying it's her? It's someone who looks like her. It is not her.

SANTHOSH. You can see her . . . face.

MALINI (*shaking her head*). It's someone else.

SANTHOSH. It's very clear who she is.

MALINI. It's not – it can be any girl in the uniform. It can be any schoolgirl with long curly hair, h-how did you get it?

SANTHOSH. Jeevan gave it to me.

MALINI. How did he get it?

SANTHOSH. Jeevan shot it.

MALINI. How could he – how could you let your son, what sort of a son have you got? Where does he get such ideas from?

SANTHOSH. I don't know.

MALINI. It doesn't look like her. If it does, it's because, it's been digitally, her face has been morphed.

SANTHOSH. I came here because I thought you knew about it, because this is a dangerous thing, we ought to do something about it before it's too late.

Pause. MALINI *looks at the film.*

MALINI. *Avuh illey.* [It's not her.] Her scar is not there. She fell off the wall when she was six and tore her skin. She has a scar.

She has a scar on her left . . .

She sees the scar. Silence.

It's nothing. Scars can be digitally, everything can be digitally . . .

SANTHOSH. Perhaps I should turn on the volume –

MALINI. No! (*Pause.*) No.

Pause.

SANTHOSH. Did she get twenty-four in her botany test? Did she?
She mentions that . . . at some point.

Silence.

MALINI. You watched the whole thing?

Silence.

Switch it off, switch it off.

*He is about to step forward but she moves away from him. She
fiddles with the phone, but it won't switch off.*

Switch it off, switch it off.

SANTHOSH. It's the red button.

MALINI *switches it off. She's nearly in tears. Silence.*

Are you all right?

Silence.

MALINI. Who else has seen it? I've got to delete it. Don't come near
me, tell me how to delete it.

SANTHOSH. You press the green, go into the folder and press the
red button. Let me . . .

MALINI. No! If you tell anyone else about this, I'll kill you. *Porikki*
bastard! *Porikki* family. Cheap dirty dirty people, filthy people,
perverts, stay away from my daughter, tell your son to stay away
from my daughter, and my son, stay away from my family.
(*Crying*). How c . . . This . . . Idiot, stupid stupid girl.

She cries.

He is not in it. He isn't there? She is there but he isn't?

SANTHOSH. I'm sorry.

Pause.

18

MALINI. Has . . . has anyone else seen it?

SANTHOSH. Yes. Arjun. He's in Jeevan's class.

MALINI. Did you speak to him?

SANTHOSH. No. He's still in class.

MALINI. You'll have to catch him soon and get him to keep quiet about it. (*Pause*.) Will you do it?

SANTHOSH. It's a little complicated.

MALINI. What do you mean?

SANTHOSH. Jeevan said he forwarded it only to Arjun. But Arjun, apparently he's forwarded it to a few boys. Jeevan said, some boys in his class were watching the film. (*Pause*.) There are other boys who have it, Mrs Haridas. But Jeevan forwarded it only to Arjun.

MALINI. *Kadavuley* [Oh, God], what has he done? How many other boys has Arjun forwarded it to?

SANTHOSH. Three or four. At the most five, six.

MALINI. We need to get hold of them. We need to get them to delete the film. Do you know who those boys are?

SANTHOSH. No. Not yet.

MALINI. Not yet? Not yet?

SANTHOSH. I'm on it. These things take time, but it's not hard. It's like tracking down customers who won't pay up.

MALINI. Does the principal know?

SANTHOSH. No. At least, not yet.

MALINI. That's good, that's good. Who else knows about it?

Pause.

SANTHOSH. Your son. He gave Jeevan a black eye yesterday.

Pause.

MALINI. I want every single film deleted by tomorrow. I want this done before, before . . . I want every single one of them gone.

SANTHOSH. Don't order me about. My son is also involved. I'm just as concerned about it as you.

19

MALINI. What has he gone and done? If word gets out, it's my daughter who will be destroyed, not your son. If that film is not deleted, Mr Santhosh Kumar, I will go to the police. I will file a case against your son. Of assault. Do you understand?

SHARAN *enters. Silence.*

SHARAN. Amma? Do you know? Ma?

MALINI. You tell me!

SHARAN. Deepa's class teacher asked me to bring her cycle home.

MALINI *doesn't respond.*

Ma?

MALINI *turns to him with aggression.* SHARAN *steps back.*

(*To* SANTHOSH.) What do you want? Why are you here?

SANTHOSH. Your mother and I had – things to discuss.

SHARAN. I thought he was my friend. I trusted him. He's a bastard, he's a freaking bastard. Get the fuck out!

SANTHOSH. Mind your tongue, boy! (*Pause.*) Look. I'm sorry. But your sister, she's no innocent in all this. She didn't say no. You must understand that. (*Pause. To* MALINI.) My son says, he insists they had safe sex. There's no chance of pregnancy. But if there's some slip-up, do what you have to. Only don't involve me.

SANTHOSH *leaves, taking his cellphone with him. Silence. Water lorry hoots.* MALINI *doesn't move.*

MALINI. You knew. You knew the two were seeing each other.

SHARAN. I didn't –

MALINI. Don't lie.

SHARAN. I'm not. They never told me.

MALINI. But you knew.

Water lorry hoots.

SHARAN. The water lorry –

MALINI. You knew about the cellphone.

Silence.

20

SHARAN. You wouldn't have believed me if I'd told you. You wouldn't have heard a word against her.

MALINI. You didn't even try. (*Silence*.) Where's your cellphone? Are you deaf? Where is it?

SHARAN gives it to her. MALINI takes it.

No more cellphones from now on.

MALINI picks up a dustbin and takes it to where the plastic bag of the previous scene is. In a frenzy she opens the bag and combs through the contents. She dumps all lipsticks, nail polish, kohl, baubles in the dustbin.

SHARAN. Ma. What are you doing?

MALINI. These are what made her . . .

He tries to approach her but doesn't. She takes the notebooks and flips the pages to find any slip of paper hidden between the pages. She finds a photograph of Jeevan, which she rips to pieces. She finds a Mills and Boon novel, which she tries to rip. When she's unable to rip it, she is close to tears. She dumps the book as it is in the bin. She gets SHARAN's hockey stick from the shoe rack. SHARAN is clearly scared. She goes to the set-top box (that receives cable channels).

SHARAN. Ma! It's, it cost us 5000!

She keeps the set-top box and hockey stick in the cupboard. She goes after the video-game console.

That's mine, Ma! I didn't do anything.

She dumps it in the cupboard and locks it, taking the key with her.

She goes to the kitchen and comes out with a knife.

Please, you are scaring me.

She cuts the plug off the TV.

MALINI. No TV. No movies. No games. No entertainment. No distraction. No nothing.

SHARAN. What did I do?

She tears away the posters on the wall.

MALINI. He was your friend. (*Tear.*) She was your sister. (*Tear.*) You should have stopped it. (*Tear.*) You knew about the MMS. (*Tear.*) You didn't say a word.

She goes to the drawers and finds a pair of scissors. She walks into Deepa's room. SHARAN stays. Water lorry hoots.

Scene Four

Friday. 10.30 am. MALINI and RAMESH. MALINI is very upset, which she's trying to cover up by being overly cheerful. Books, pencil, eraser on the floor — signs that they've been flung. MALINI has some forms in her hands. As they move towards the sofa, MALINI spots a notebook on the floor, which she picks up. RAMESH picks up a pencil and gives it to MALINI.

MALINI. So sorry, everything's such a mess here.

MALINI puts away notebook and pencil.

You really needn't have gone through all this trouble – you could have couriered.

RAMESH. But this is faster. I knew you could do with the cheque at a time like this.

MALINI. Thanks.

RAMESH. Diseases like this take their time.

MALINI. Yes. That's right. Well. (*Laughs.*) This is quite a lot of paper.

RAMESH. You have to fill up in triplicate.

MALINI scans the forms. RAMESH gives her a pen. She begins to fill them in. Silence.

You must be anxious. How to get her married off if the marks don't fade.

MALINI. Believe me, that's the least of my worries.

RAMESH looks around. He picks up a textbook on the floor.

RAMESH. *Botany is Fun for Higher Secondary.*

MALINI (*beat*). It's, a, a – yes. (*Laughs*.) Nothing's where it should be. This house looks like a disaster zone.

RAMESH. This house looks like someone in it has measles.

MALINI. It says here I need a doctor's certificate.

RAMESH. Give it when you get back to work. (*Silence*.) So many books. There's too much pressure on kids these days. It wasn't like that when we were young.

MALINI. *Ennuh* [What] pressure? I don't force them. They do things on their own. (*Pause*.) Is it wrong to want them to do well, so they can be someone when they grow up?

RAMESH. *Illelle* [no, no] –

MALINI. She wanted to do medicine. It wasn't my idea – though now she says it's mine. She wanted to take part in those competitions. I didn't ask her to. Is being happy when she gets prizes pressure?

RAMESH. You got me wrong –

MALINI. Whatever the pressure, all kids go through them.

RAMESH. I meant, the school system. It is all wrong.

Silence.

Page three-*le oru* signature.

MALINI. Who'll tell them that?

RAMESH. Sorry?

MALINI. The school authorities? That they're at fault? Schools-*laan* don't keep an eye on children. You see, they spend eight hours every day in school and that's without taking into account special classes and evening games. That's far more time there than at home. Correct, *dhaaney* [isn't it]? But are schools willing to take responsibility?

Silence.

RAMESH. What did the doctor say?

MALINI. Unh? He said she'll get better.

RAMESH. It'll take a month at least for the disease to run its course.

MALINI. Or more. I don't know. It's her body!

Silence.

RAMESH. Can I have some water?

MALINI. Why don't I get you some juice.

RAMESH. *Ille*, water is f –

MALINI. I'll get us all some orange juice.

MALINI *gets two juice cartons.* RAMESH *and* MALINI *drink.*

Was – Nair in a terrible mood?

RAMESH. Yes.

MALINI. It was my leave, *le*? Maybe I should call him up and explain.

RAMESH. Don't worry. He'll get over it. I'll take care of it. He – he listens to me. For some reason, he respects my judgement.

Silence.

MALINI. Illnesses don't make an appointment and come for me to plan in advance. Wouldn't I have told him if I'd known?

RAMESH. Even my coming here was a spur of the moment thing.

Pause.

MALINI. Did Nair send you here to check on me?

RAMESH. No! Why would you think that? I came to see you, to help you – I wanted to because you are all alone. (*Pause.*) I should have phoned and come, but I thought good deeds don't require a call.

MALINI. They don't. I'm sorry.

RAMESH. I can come by later. Or as you said, you could use the courier fellows.

MALINI. It's – her illness. It's . . . already Shakti Complex-*le,* two children have rashes all over. Do you know that?

RAMESH. Is that so? Soon every child down the street will have it. That's how times are. One child catches a cold, then in an instant, every child in the country is sneezing. (*Pause.*) Neem.

MALINI. Sorry?

RAMESH. Neem leaves are good for skin rashes. My mother says so.

SHARAN *enters. He is very upset.*

Hello. School closed early today?

MALINI. He has exams next week – *adhaan* [that is why] half a day today. Neem, huh?

SHARAN *goes to Deepa's room. He tries to open it. It's locked from the inside.*

RAMESH. Yes. I can get some tomorrow on my way to work.

MALINI. Sorry?

RAMESH. We have a neem tree near our building.

MALINI. Oh, we have one in our colony too. Thanks.

SHARAN *rattles the door.*

RAMESH (*to* MALINI). Isn't it better for sick children to keep their doors unlocked?

MALINI. What? She – she's used to – force of habit. Children these days! (*Laughs.*) We need visas to enter their rooms. Especially mothers.

SHARAN. I want to talk to you! Let me in!

RAMESH *laughs.* MALINI *tries to laugh.* SHARAN *bangs on the door.*

MALINI. Sharan! We have a guest! Stop it, all right!

SHARAN. They said – They can't – She ruined everything!

MALINI. They, they were supposed to – do a project together. Juniors and seniors. A science project.

SHARAN *bangs on door.*

Calm down!

SHARAN. I was studying all month – I could have got ninety this time. What's going to happen now?

MALINI. It's – just a project!

RAMESH. Relax. You can't find a solution if you panic. Isn't that right?

MALINI. Unh? Yes, yes. At their age, every little problem gets amplified a hundred times.

SHARAN. You said Santhosh Uncle would take care of everything –

MALINI. Shh . . . please – you'll aggravate her illness.

RAMESH. Uncle? I didn't know you had a family.

MALINI. What? I don't.

SHARAN. Ask the bitch to set it all right!

MALINI *slaps him half-heartedly.*

MALINI. Listen, please. *Okkaru da!* [Sit down!] Why don't you, why don't you go to your room and and . . .

SHARAN *shrugs her away.*

RAMESH. Santhosh? Who's he?

SHARAN. He's run away. They've all run away. Gone off to Sri Lanka or Canada.

MALINI. What?

RAMESH. Why is he absconding? Has he stolen anything?

MALINI. No, no. Not stolen.

SHARAN. You said he'll sort it all out.

RAMESH. What sort of uncle?

MALINI. I do have a – I have a brother in the States. But he's not. I mean Santhosh is not my brother. He's a, a, someone we, his son studies with my . . . (*Tries to laugh.*) I can't really make head or tail out of this. (*To* SHARAN.) We'll talk about it later.

SHARAN. They're getting away with everything. How can they get away?

RAMESH. Has that man cheated you? I have friends in the police.

MALINI. That won't be necessary. Calm down!

RAMESH. Is he coming down with measles too?

MALINI. He – he looks pale. Doesn't he? First – let's, let me finish these . . .

MALINI *gives the forms back to* RAMESH.

RAMESH. You've not signed.

She takes back the forms. Her hands are shaking. She signs.

It's only a project. It's not the boards.

MALINI *laughs.*

SHARAN. If Appa were alive none of this would have freaking happened.

RAMESH. I like this. A son's utter faith in his father to stop viruses. Diseases come and diseases go, young man. (*Beat.*) But a man's presence can be helpful sometimes.

MALINI. There! All done!

MALINI *gives him the forms.*

RAMESH. Right.

MALINI. It's getting late. Nair must be wondering where you are.

RAMESH. Well. If there's anything I can do . . . *edhaavadhu* [anything].

MALINI. I'll call you.

RAMESH. Will you?

MALINI. Yes.

RAMESH. I nearly forgot your cheque.

MALINI *laughs.* RAMESH *gives her the cheque. He exits. Silence.*

SHARAN (*at Deepa's door*). Look what you've done! Look what you've done to me!

MALINI. Tell me what happened?

SHARAN. They've expelled us.

MALINI. Us?

SHARAN. Me and her. And Jeevan. I didn't do anything.

MALINI. Expelled or suspended?

SHARAN. Expelled.

SHARAN *takes a letter from his pocket. He gives it to* MALINI.

MALINI *reads*. SHARAN *paces*.

MALINI. 'For obscene behaviour.'

SHARAN. It's on the net now.

MALINI. On the net!

SHARAN. People are buying it off the net. A Tamil paper wrote about it and Princi found out. It was this small, somewhere in the inside pages. She showed it to me. It said teenagers were having sex because it was all a big adventure. Why am I being punished for what she did?

Silence.

MALINI. On the net!

SHARAN. For 200 bucks. You said I could fight this if I get good marks. Jeevan is clever. He escaped. He'll start afresh in Sri Lanka or Canada. He'll become an engineer. He'll be all right.

MALINI *reads the letter again*.

No matter how many times you read it, it'll say the same thing.

MALINI. On the net!

SHARAN. Why the hell can't we run away too? Why can't we start from scratch? (*Silence*.) Everyone in school knows what she did. I can't ever go back. I have maths exams next week. I've been slogging over trigonometry the whole of this month. Make her set it right. Tell her to set it all right. (*Silence*.) Tell her I'll kill her. Tell your little whore I'll – kill her!

Scene Five

Friday. 5.30 pm. SHARAN *and* MALINI. *Deepa's door bolted from the outside*. SHARAN *is in front of the computer*. MALINI *removes her green dupatta. It is torn. She wraps a towel around her like a shawl*.

SHARAN. Maybe they didn't have a chance to take your picture. You said you'd covered your face with your dupatta. Maybe they don't know who you are. Maybe they're taking everyone else's –

MALINI. They know me.

SHARAN. What if –

MALINI. They've joined the dots. How far have you got?

SHARAN. A few more minutes.

MALINI *reaches out for the mouse.* SHARAN *stops her.*

MALINI. *Pinnuh* [Then] hurry up!

MALINI *goes to the table. She pours some water into a glass.*

What? I know, all right? It's only half a glass.

From this point onwards, from time to time, MALINI *dips the edge of her towel into the glass and rubs the exposed parts of her body clean.*

SHARAN. I can't work without a surname.

MALINI. I told you. He was always S. Balan here.

SHARAN. S for . . . ?

MALINI. Shankar.

SHARAN. Shankar Balan. Nothing.

MALINI. Try Balan Shankar.

SHARAN *shakes his head.*

What about Balan Shankar-an?

SHARAN. No.

MALINI. Sankaran. S-A- not S-H-A-. (*Pause.*) What?

SHARAN (*trying to cheer her up*). I can't believe there'd be so many ways the name can be spelt! Shankar with an 'h' Sankar without an 'h'. Shankaran with an 'h', Sankaran without an 'h'. And if some astrologer has asked him to follow numerology or something – we are screwed. Ah? There's a Balan with four As. What do you say to that, huh? (*Pause.*) What will you say to him? Will he talk to you? Seventeen years is a long time to stay angry with one's sister.

MALINI. He's Tamil. He can carry a grudge into his next birth.

SHARAN. Just because Appa belonged to a different community?

MALINI. Oh, wouldn't he love to see me grovel?

SHARAN. There's Shanckar with a 'ck' now!

MALINI. Maybe he's Balllan with a 'triple-l'?

SHARAN (*laughs*). Or Zhanqar with a 'zq'?

MALINI. Or Pshankar with a silent 'p'.

They smile. Silence.

SHARAN. Ma. It's okay, you know. It's not like I need to go to school.

MALINI *turns away abruptly.*

MALINI. *Chumma olaraadhey.* [Don't talk nonsense.] You need an
education. Finished?

SHARAN. I need to filter this. Where in America?

MALINI. Don't know.

SHARAN. Do you know which university he went to?

MALINI. No.

SHARAN. Which subject?

MALINI. Maths. That's what he got a scholarship for. But he could
have done something else in the States.

SHARAN. Date of birth?

MALINI. October 26, 1967.

SHARAN. Does he have a wife?

MALINI. He may. He's likely to have a family now. Though I can't
see him as a family man. He's far too self-absorbed.

SHARAN. So that's where Deepa gets it from!

MALINI (*snaps*). Well?

SHARAN. Almost there, almost there.

SHARAN *types. Bell rings. The two don't move. It rings again and
again.*

VOICE (*off*). Mrs Haridas. Are you in there? Mrs Haridas? We are
from Theta TV. We'd like to speak to you for a moment. We'd like
your side of the story.

Bell rings. Then silence. MALINI *goes to the peephole, looks into it.*

SHARAN (*whispers*). Are they still there?

MALINI *nods*.

VOICE (*off*). You can call us anytime. You'll find the number on our channel.

Silence.

SHARAN (*whispers*). What if we talk to them?

MALINI. What? Are you mad? After what they did to me? All those dirty hands, filthy groping hands, thrusting cameras in my face, taunting me, tearing my dupatta – you must be joking!

SHARAN. Maybe they won't be that – violent if we voluntarily talk to / them.

MALINI. Voluntarily? Do you have any idea what you're saying? They'll think they have the right to claw at our flesh, to rip us into shreds, and do whatever they want with us. I can't let that happen. No. We have to stay out of the media glare.

SHARAN. Ma?

MALINI (*snaps*). *Ennuh da?* [What?]

SHARAN. Nothing.

MALINI. Then shut up and do your work!

SHARAN. I told you not to go. I told you I saw some people with cameras. I told you the principal wouldn't take me back. You wouldn't listen.

Silence.

Are you feeling cold?

MALINI. I'm . . . Just focus for once, all right?

Pause. A letter slides from under Deepa's door.

SHARAN. If Appa were alive, he'd have found a way to get us out of here . . . Do you think of him?

MALINI. Of course. Every time I think of him, I curse him.

SHARAN. Ma!

MALINI. Well, what do you expect? I shouldn't be the one left to deal with this ordeal all alone.

SHARAN. He died.

MALINI (*beat*). He shouldn't have. (*Pause.*) Well?

SHARAN. It's processing.

> SHARAN *gets up. He's seen the letter.* MALINI *goes to the computer and waits.* SHARAN *goes to Deepa's door, picks up the letter, glances at it and tears it.* MALINI *turns at the noise.* SHARAN *pushes the pieces back under Deepa's door. Silence.*

> (*Loudly.*) She never thinks about anyone else but her. You never saw that, did you?

> *Pause.*

MALINI. Twenty-three in all.

SHARAN. She says she regrets it. It's too goddamn late for all that. Are you going to call now? It's pretty early there.

> MALINI *takes the telephone and plugs it in. It begins to ring.* MALINI *hesitates. She picks it up. It's a lewd call.*

MALINI. Bastard pervert guttermouth. The police is tracing this call.

> SHARAN *smiles.* MALINI *bangs down the receiver. The moment she lifts her finger off the phone, it rings again.* MALINI *disconnects it again. She keeps the receiver off the hook. She looks at the computer.*

> He'd be annoyed – and unreasonable if I call him all of a sudden. He'd rake old things up. (*Pause.*) He was such a, a stubborn man.

> *Pause.*

> He said marrying your father would be a disaster. He said I wouldn't amount to much with him for a husband.

> *A pause before she looks at the computer and calls the number.*

> Hi. I'm calling from India. I'm looking for my brother Balan Shankaran? . . . I don't know. It's . . . it's about 5.30 in the evening here . . . 4.30 in the morning? I'm so sorry . . . My name is Malini. I'm calling from India. I'm looking for my brother Balan Shankaran. He's from Coimbatore . . . Are you Mr Balan Shankaran? . . . I don't understand. You are mistaken. I'm not from a call centre. I'm looking for my —

Pause. MALINI *replaces the receiver. Phone rings.* MALINI *lets it ring. She rubs her face with the towel.*

SHARAN. Bloody bastards!

SHARAN *disconnects the phone and keeps the receiver off the hook.* MALINI *rubs her face.*

MALINI. Next number *ennuh* [what]?

SHARAN *goes back to the computer. He clicks.*

SHARAN. If we get hold of Balan Mama, will I have to repeat a year again in America? Will the subjects be different? Will I go to school on a skateboard?

No response from MALINI.

Do you think people would really not know her there? What if they do? You said, you said there was no such thing as far away with a cellphone. What if Balan Mama says no? (*Silence.*) What if he's watched it?

MALINI. What do you want me to say, unh? What the hell do you want me to say? I don't have the energy or the inclination to make you feel better. If you feel hungry, fix yourself something to eat. If you feel sad, go hug yourself. But don't expect anything from me. Understand? Next number *ennuh*? Oh, stop wasting my time! Give me that!

MALINI *pushes* SHARAN *away and clicks on the computer herself.* SHARAN *watches her. He reaches out to hug her, but doesn't.*

Scene Six

Saturday. 10 pm. RAMESH, SHARAN *and* MALINI. RAMESH *gives* MALINI *two bottles of water.*

RAMESH. I wanted to get here as soon as you called, but I could manage only now. I saw the lights on and knew you weren't asleep. Sorry, it's not Bisleri.

MALINI. This is just what we need. Thank you.

MALINI *drinks a little from a bottle.* SHARAN *takes the other bottle and drinks. Then* SHARAN *unlatches Deepa's door, goes inside and comes back without the bottle.* RAMESH *tries to catch a glimpse of Deepa.* SHARAN *immediately closes the door and bolts it.* SHARAN *pretends to go to his desk and sort out his books. He keeps an eye on the adults.*

RAMESH. Was that . . . her? She doesn't look anything like you, does she?

MALINI. Well. She –

RAMESH. Or him. (*Pause.*) When I watched the nine o'clock news yesterday, I knew you'd call me. I had a sixth sense about it. You are on all the channels, do you know that? (*Pause.*) Sorry. I think I should have lied.

MALINI. *Che che.* Honesty is fine.

RAMESH. Green is not your colour.

MALINI. I'll keep that in mind.

RAMESH. It's shocking. What she did, it's not normal. Apparently, these are early indications of (*Looks to see if* SHARAN *is looking at him.*) nymphomania. Really. It should be nipped in the bud. Yesterday, on TV, a psychologist was saying that Indian teenagers are getting (*Beat.*) active at a very young age. Apparently, it's to do with their diet. It's because they're switching over from *thayir saadam* [curd rice] to pizza.

MALINI. She eats *thayir saadam* every day.

RAMESH. Then it must be something else.

MALINI. Ramesh. The reason I called –

RAMESH. Coffee perhaps? It's known to have aphrodisiac properties. Really.

MALINI *is uncomfortable.*

How do kids know what to do, do you think? (*Laughs.*) I've never talked to a woman like this about all these things before.

SHARAN *plonks himself near* RAMESH *and stares at him. The adults are uncomfortable. Silence.*

(*To* SHARAN.) There were so many media people. Then there were the women with broomsticks. Women from the slums, women

34

in starched saris. Did you watch it? They were sweeping your street, every inch of it. (*To* MALINI.) I have upset you, haven't I?

MALINI. *Kadavuley!* [Oh, God!] They are here? But we are decent people.

RAMESH. It's that sort of a crime. I thought your brother would be here with you.

MALINI. He – he's in America. He couldn't – No, it's not like that at all – he just lost his job, and he can't . . . help us. Us going there or him coming here, that is out of the question.

RAMESH*'s phone beeps; he's got a message.* RAMESH *ignores it.*

You are such a nice – you seem to – what I mean is, you'll know someone who . . . Would you like something to drink?

RAMESH. Water?

MALINI. Of course. Sharan?

SHARAN *gets up reluctantly and pours a little water into a glass for* RAMESH.

(*To* RAMESH.) This is getting a little . . . we really need to . . .

SHARAN *gives* RAMESH *the glass.* SHARAN *is clumsy, pouring a little water on* RAMESH*'s shirt.* RAMESH *takes out his cellphone from the pocket and begins to wipe it dry with a handkerchief.*

Ennuh idhu? [What is this?] Can't you be more careful?

SHARAN. Sorry.

RAMESH (*to* SHARAN *who's staring at the phone now*). It's a Nokia.

MALINI. We have to leave this place, Ramesh. (*To* SHARAN.) Just stop – stop crowding me, all right?

Pause.

SHARAN. Where do you want me to go?

SHARAN *moves away.*

Is this far enough for you? Or I could go downstairs. Do you want me to do that?

RAMESH. Listen –

SHARAN. You are not the only one worrying, you know?

MALINI. Am I supposed to rejoice that I have company? Can I have a moment to myself without you breathing down my neck? Unh? Go away, Sharan.

SHARAN. Me. Or her? You can't suddenly decide you don't want us.

MALINI. I don't have time for all this right now. Just go away.

SHARAN. I freaking won't.

MALINI. Sorry about that.

RAMESH. I don't understand. What's wrong with this flat?

MALINI. I – we need to hide somewhere.

Pause.

RAMESH. This flat is perfectly – it's absolutely all right. It's safe.

MALINI. Is it?

RAMESH. It's inside a colony. (*Pause.*) I doubt if I can be of any help. It's not so easy, you know that. You are a notorious figure now. I'd offer you my home, but I live in a joint family. It's not just me. I have to ask my *anna*'s [elder brother] permission, and I don't think he'll give it. And my mother, she's very set in her ways. She doesn't appreciate guests.

MALINI. I wasn't asking that of you.

RAMESH. I thought I should tell you anyway.

MALINI. That's –

RAMESH. Don't mistake me.

MALINI. I don't.

RAMESH. She – watches TV all day.

MALINI. Right. Right. (*To* SHARAN.) Do you want something?

SHARAN. No.

Pause.

RAMESH. This really is a lovely little flat.

MALINI. Actually, I was hoping you'd ask around. Ask friends may be.

RAMESH. Oh. Sure.

MALINI. A friend with a flat or, or a house or a – a farm house, away from the city, away from prying eyes. I thought you may know someone who can loan us a place for a while – A month or two – till all this dies down. We can't afford much – all my savings went into their education. My credit card, it's overdrawn already. I thought you may have friends. Rich friends who'll not consider my – our – history.

Pause.

RAMESH. Is that why you called me here?

MALINI. No, no, no. You are such a, a pillar kind of a person. You know, solid. Not physically.

RAMESH. I do have a friend. (*Pause.*) Murugan. I'll ask him.

MALINI *nods.*

He's likely to have a space – a, a cottage or something. A villa, a flat, he's the type to invest in real estate. He's – a good friend. I'll speak to him.

MALINI. Thank you. Today itself?

RAMESH. It's a bit late. First thing tomorrow morning.

Stones are thrown at a window in the kitchen. Sound of glass breaking. Laughter outside. MALINI rushes to the kitchen. RAMESH follows her, somewhat afraid. SHARAN nearly follows them but sees the cellphone on the table. He picks it up and scans it furtively. RAMESH re-enters.

Both windows are gone.

RAMESH sees SHARAN fiddling with his phone. SHARAN instinctively replaces the phone back on the table. Pause.

SHARAN. So. Do you really have friends who can help us? (*Pause.*) My mother said you don't have friends. She said you eat in the office canteen all alone. Is that true? (*Pause.*) She said you were pathetic. She said your hair smells of cheap dye.

RAMESH moves forward to pick up his phone. SHARAN takes it and moves away. SHARAN begins to check it, evading RAMESH.

MALINI. Sharan, help me with the shards. (*Pause.*) What's going on?

RAMESH. What sort of children have you brought up? He calls me all sorts of names. Now he's taken away my cellphone.

MALINI. What's the meaning of this? Give it back to him. You're not a child any more. Behave yourself!

RAMESH. Give it back.

SHARAN *freezes*.

SHARAN. You sick, sick bastard.

SHARAN *shows* MALINI *the phone*.

Sick sick sick sick . . .

RAMESH. I don't know what he's talking about.

SHARAN. I knew it. I knew he had it all along.

RAMESH. Honestly! I don't know what –

SHARAN. He has it, Ma. He has her. See it for yourself.

RAMESH. Malini! I have no idea how it got there. I didn't – it must be a new message. This must be the message I got a few minutes ago. You heard the beep. Someone must have sent – everybody gets these things. It's all over the place. I didn't even know it was there, if I had, I'd have deleted it, I'm a god-fearing man. Deepa is like a daughter to me.

SHARAN. Ask him if he's watched her.

RAMESH. No! I haven't. *Paaru* [Look], Malini. I came here, because I wanted to help. I brought you water. I was about to talk to Murugan for you. I didn't expect this, the boy's gone mad!

SHARAN. You are nothing but a dirty old lying bastard! Get out! Get the hell out of my house!

MALINI. That's enough! Apologise at once!

SHARAN. Ma?

MALINI. I heard his phone beep.

SHARAN. He has the MMS –

MALINI (*to* RAMESH). Don't get angry. He's only a boy, he doesn't know what he does or says half the time. I'm so sorry – I apologise on his behalf. Please.

SHARAN. He's a paedophile.

MALINI *slaps him*.

RAMESH. This is too much, I say! There is a limit to my patience! I came to help you and I get abused in return?

MALINI. No! Don't go! Enough! Go inside! Go to your room now! Ramesh is an honourable man. I'll not hear a word against him. Is that clear? Is that clear?

Scene Seven

Sunday. 9 pm. MALINI, SHARAN *and* KOKILA. *Sounds of lewd singing from outside.* SHARAN *ignores* MALINI. *He plays with an empty bottle.*

KOKILA. I know it is late. I do not normally disturb people when they are sleeping –

MALINI. *Paravaayille* [That's all right], Kokila – We weren't asleep.

KOKILA. Your kitchen windows are broken.

MALINI. Oh, we'll replace them – we'll get better ones.

KOKILA. This is all very alarming. The crowd's getting bigger and bigger. We can't go out. Water lorries can't get in. It's the third day we've not been able to fill water.

MALINI. I know – Please bear with us for a bit more.

KOKILA. For how much longer, Malini? We've not had a drop to drink all evening. I've not been able to cook anything today. No rice, no sambar. We've run out of bread and dry food. We can't even go out to buy some more.

MALINI. This situation – it can't last very long. They all have to leave at some point.

KOKILA. My husband was not able to go to his office. He's getting a salary cut now for taking leave. Keshav was not able to go to school yesterday. We've had no post, no courier the last three days. *Porum pa!* [Enough!] We can't go through another day like this. We need water. What are you going to do about it?

MALINI. We called the police yesterday.

KOKILA. They never came. They'll not come also. They'll come after everything is over. Like in Tamil movies.

MALINI. Please don't be angry.

KOKILA. How can I not be? Why should fifty-nine families suffer because of one wayward family?

MALINI. Deepa made a mistake –

KOKILA. Telling a lie, *adhu oru* mistake. Or being rude. But this is more than a mistake.

MALINI. She's really sorry for all that has happened. We all are.

Silence.

KOKILA. *Ennuh aachu avanukku?* [What's the matter with him?] Is he all right?

MALINI. What? Yes.

KOKILA. He looks like his ship has overturned. Is there some water in that bottle? (*Pause.*) Sharan?

SHARAN. No.

KOKILA *looks at* MALINI.

KOKILA. It sounded as if there was a little left in the bottle.

MALINI. Sharan?

SHARAN *ignores them. He plays with the bottle.* MALINI *goes to* SHARAN *and takes the bottle away. The bottle is empty.* SHARAN *moves away from* MALINI. *He finds another empty bottle to play with.*

KOKILA. This afternoon, people paraded her effigy on a donkey. Actually, all of your effigies. (*Pointing to* SHARAN.) Even yours. I saw it all on TV. The women and their broomsticks . . . political parties are getting involved. The watchman ran away this evening. We have no security now. (*Pause.*) My *manni* [sister-in-law] called from Delhi last night and asked why I have allowed disreputable people inside the colony. I didn't know what to say to her! We can't show our faces outside the colony any more. Already two families are vacating Shakti Complex.

MALINI. What do you want me to do?

KOKILA. It's not an issue of what I want. It's what the residents want.

Bell rings. SHARAN goes to the peephole and looks. Bell rings again and again. He shakes his head and returns.

This has never happened before, never once in Shakti Complex. Now all sorts of lumpens are coming and ringing our doorbells and harassing us. (*Pause.*) Tomorrow we are holding an emergency meeting to decide on a course of action. (*Pause.*) Is there some place you can go to, a relative's place or something?

SHARAN. Do you want us to leave?

MALINI (*laughs nervously*). She's not saying that. She thinks we'll be safer with a relative. Isn't that so?

KOKILA (*beat*). You said you had a brother or a sister.

MALINI shakes her head.

MALINI. We have no one. Only friends. Like you.

KOKILA. Do you realise the kind of ordeal you are putting us through? All of us, we are trying not to use the loo too much. Still our flats have started to stink. Our homes are filthy. We can't take it any more. The residents have been calling me all day, telling me to take action.

MALINI. Kokila, please. Where will we go? We need your help. Listen, I'm looking for a place to hide, a place where the children will be safe, but we need time for that. Please talk to the residents. They'll listen to you.

KOKILA. Frank-*aa solren* [I'll speak frankly]. There's little I can do when there's all sorts of talk flying about the town. One paper even says she's gone and contracted AIDS.

MALINI. That's ridiculous! You don't believe that!

KOKILA. *Che!* No! Don't I know what is true and what is not? (*Pause.*) I read somewhere she eloped with that boy.

MALINI laughs.

MALINI. She's right here. *Andhuh* room-*le*. Really.

KOKILA. I am only repeating what I'm hearing in the news.

SHARAN. She's studying.

KOKILA. What's the point now? (*Pause.*) What was that? That . . . noise? Was that Deepa? (*Pause.*) There's another matter. (*Pause.*) You had a male visitor yesterday.

MALINI. Oh. Ramesh. He's my colleague.

KOKILA (*to* SHARAN). He climbed our wall to get in. You didn't know that, did you?

MALINI. He couldn't use the gate. Oh, but he was only trying to help me. (*To* SHARAN *and* KOKILA.) He's an upright man.

KOKILA. A man climbs a wall in the dead of the night to meet a woman. What will people make of that? (*To* MALINI.) This is a colony of decent familes.

MALINI. Kokila – you know me. You've known me since the kids were toddlers. You know I'm not like that. Ramesh, he – he works daytime. He bought Super Sparkler from us the other day. Ask Sharan.

SHARAN *does not respond. He continues to play with the bottle.*

KOKILA. Ah. That's another thing. Rumours are flying left and right. One paper says the powder business you do, that's a front.

MALINI. A front for what?

KOKILA. For unsavoury business. I don't believe that, but some people might. You may think you are free to do whatever you want because you don't have a husband. But you must remember you have children.

MALINI. He came because I called him. I have no one else to turn to.

Pause.

SHARAN. Aunty, he won't come again.

MALINI. You have no business –

SHARAN. I promise you.

MALINI. How dare you! This is my concern. Don't interfere. Understand?

Pause.

SHARAN (*to* KOKILA). Tell her, I have eyes. Tell her, I can see.

MALINI. You saw all wrong.

SHARAN. Tell her, she's being as foolish as her.

MALINI. Enough! Go – go and see if we have some water left.

KOKILA. Do you?

SHARAN. No.

MALINI. We must have a little bit of water somewhere.

SHARAN. Aunty, we don't.

Pause.

KOKILA. All this talking . . . my throat is dry.

SHARAN *leaves. Long silence.*

MALINI. Sorry about that. He was way out of line.

KOKILA. I always thought you backed the wrong horse, Malini.

MALINI. What do you mean?

KOKILA. I saw the way you were with both. I think you've not been fair to him.

MALINI. That's absurd. I treated them both equally.

KOKILA. That's my humble opinion.

Silence.

Is she talking to herself? It's strange. You had to pry her mouth open to get a few words out of her. Now it flows in a torrent when there's no one to listen to her.

Pause.

MALINI. I'll speak to the residents. We'll come up with something if we all put our heads together –

KOKILA. They don't want you at the meeting when they're discussing you.

SHARAN *returns.*

SHARAN. I'm sorry. We have totally run out of water.

KOKILA. And we are running out of time.

Pause.

SHARAN. What if we can make the crowd leave?

KOKILA. How?

SHARAN. Will you let us stay then?

KOKILA. How?

SHARAN. I don't know. But will you?

KOKILA. Do you have a game plan? Otherwise, no point speculating.

SHARAN. What if, what if we go downstairs and speak to the people?

MALINI. They want only one thing: our blood. They won't leave unless they get it.

Pause.

KOKILA. I sympathise, I really do. I wish I can help but I have to worry about my own family. Also fifty-eight others.

KOKILA *gets up to leave.*

MALINI. Wait a minute! I think we must have a little water left somewhere. Just wait here, Kokila. *Orey nimisham.* [One minute.] I'll be right with you.

MALINI *searches.* SHARAN *follows her every move.*

Have you hidden it somewhere?

I know I didn't finish the last bottle. (*Suspiciously.*) Is it in the kitchen?

MALINI *leaves.*

KOKILA. You are the man in charge now. Ask yourself why some people are climbing the wall to get here when the whole world is spitting at you.

Silence. MALINI comes back in. Pause. She goes into Deepa's room. SHARAN rushes behind her. Seconds later, MALINI and SHARAN come out. SHARAN has a bottle that he refuses to part with. MALINI pulls at it.

MALINI. Give me.

SHARAN. It's her quota!

MALINI. Even she didn't say a word. Then what's your problem?

MALINI *snatches the bottle from* SHARAN's *hands. The bottle is only a quarter full.*

(*To* KOKILA.) I didn't realise we still had a bit. She always has a little in her room. She keeps it under her bed.

MALINI *pours the water into a glass and gives it to* KOKILA.

KOKILA. I . . . my husband has not had a drop either. We're also conserving. For Keshav.

KOKILA *drinks it thirstily.* SHARAN *and* MALINI *watch.* KOKILA *finishes the water, every drop of it.* KOKILA *looks at the bottle.*

MALINI. This is really all we have. You are the closest thing I have to a sister. Please speak up for me at the meeting. They'll listen to you. Tell them, tell them I'm looking at other options. Tell them please not to take any drastic action.

Silence.

I have my rights too, as a tenant. I'll need three months' notice.

KOKILA. These are extraordinary circumstances. None of the residents are in any mood to relent. (*Pause.*) You are asking too much from me. I'm only a secretary.

MALINI. Say you'll try.

KOKILA. I'll . . . see what I can do. (*To* SHARAN.) I've given you many buckets of water before . . . Thanks for the . . . (*Pointing to the glass. To* MALINI.) You know, for a sister, this is the first time I've been here this long in your flat. I'll call you after the meeting.

KOKILA *leaves.* MALINI *is unable to look at* SHARAN.

Scene Eight

Monday. 11 pm. MALINI *and* RAMESH. *Empty bottles.*

MALINI (*in low tone*). I thought you'd never come.

RAMESH. Sharan?

MALINI. Asleep. I was expecting you ages ago –

RAMESH. The crowd, they –

MALINI. Shh.

RAMESH. They came from nowhere.

MALINI. Are you all right?

RAMESH. For now.

MALINI. You are safe. That's what's important. You are a brave man.

RAMESH *moves away from* MALINI. *Silence.*

Did you speak to your friend?

RAMESH. He's – gone abroad for a week – *avan* [he's] jetsetter fellow.

MALINI. When will you speak to him?

RAMESH. In a day or two.

MALINI. I can't wait for a day or two. What do we do now, Ramesh?

Silence.

What is it?

Pause.

RAMESH. *Pa!* The stench . . . it's getting to me.

MALINI. You've only been here a minute.

Silence.

RAMESH. What if – what if you don't leave tomorrow?

MALINI. They'll throw us out. Kokila is already organising the men for it.

Silence.

RAMESH. What about hotels?

MALINI. Hotels?

RAMESH. It's an option.

MALINI. Can we be safe there? Can we afford them? Even if money is not the issue, how do we all get out of the colony?

Pause.

It may be easier for one person to escape than all of us. Look at it this way: with her gone, the media will leave. With the media gone, the crowd, the stragglers, the protestors – everyone will go. We will have a chance to convince Kokila to reconsider, to give us time, till we make other arrangements.

RAMESH. I can book Deepa a room.

MALINI. A girl in a hotel room – she's a sitting duck. (*Pause.*) On the other hand . . . On the other hand, with her gone . . . (*Pause.*) I can't trust anyone else to take care of her. I've thought about it long and hard. She doesn't look like the MMS girl any more. Her hair's all shorn off now. And she doesn't wear *my* [kohl] and *pottu* [bindi] and those ridiculous earrings. No one will recognise her. It's like a disguise.

RAMESH. What are you trying to say?

MALINI. Please put her up in your house. For two days. That's all. Till I make some other arrangement. She'll be safe with your family.

RAMESH. Do you realise what you're asking of me? She's soiled goods. (*Pause.*) I mean, what will people say? I'm a squeaky clean fellow, Malini. This is – how can I?

Silence.

MALINI. You are my final hope.

RAMESH. If people start connecting me with her –

MALINI. They won't, if no one warns them.

RAMESH. Listen, listen. It's not that I don't want to help – because I do. It's just that, I'm a respectable man. And she, she's beautiful – what will my mother say?

MALINI. You can say she's a colleague's daughter. That she's waiting to join her family in Dubai. That she's an unaccompanied minor and that you are her temporary guardian. You can do that.

RAMESH. I can't lie to my mother. Malini. Deepa is your burden, not mine. (*Pause.*) I was asked to stay away from you.

MALINI. From me? By your mother?

RAMESH. Yes. And by the mob. I barely escaped this time.

MALINI. Yet you are here. (*Laughs shortly.*) She keeps dragging us deeper and deeper in. I'm so glad you came back. What would I ever do –

RAMESH. I shouldn't have come.

MALINI. But you did. That means something.

SHARAN *enters.*

All these years. All these wasted years. I could have easily – I could have found a man. The loneliness. You'd know what that feels like, *le? Ille?* To come home and not have anyone to share your day with. No one to take care of you when you are sick. Nothing to look forward to . . . Please, take her with you.

RAMESH. Let me think about it –

MALINI. There's no time for that. Where is your car?

RAMESH. Near the Amman temple. There are still a lot of people roaming about, how do I take her away safely –

MALINI. We'll think of something. I'll ask her to get ready, pack a small bag.

SHARAN. Where is she going?

MALINI. God, you frightened me, sneaking up on me like that! Go back to sleep.

SHARAN. Where is she going?

MALINI. Where is who going?

SHARAN. You're sending her away with him?

MALINI. Stay away from this –

RAMESH. Did I say yes? I didn't say yes.

SHARAN. You were whoring her. How can you? She is your daughter!

MALINI. She is a whore.

SHARAN. She did something crazy. But she did it because she loved him.

MALINI. We can talk about why she did it and who is at fault all day. We don't have time. Move, Sharan. She is going with Ramesh.

MALINI *moves towards Deepa's door.* SHARAN *blocks her.*

48

SHARAN. He has her MMS.

MALINI. Everyone gets / them.

SHARAN. Don't you see? He gets a look when he talks about her.

RAMESH. What look?

MALINI. Don't be ridiculous.

RAMESH. What does he mean?

MALINI. *Olurraan.* [He's blabbering.]

SHARAN. No, no, no. She's not going anywhere with him. He's a, he's a – fucking perv.

RAMESH. How dare you!

MALINI. *Chumma iru!* [Keep quiet!] Don't talk rot!

> SHARAN *runs into Deepa's room and locks the door from the inside.*

RAMESH. I'm not . . . Is that what you think?

MALINI. I wouldn't have asked you if I'd thought that, would I? I know you better. He's a, he's not thinking straight these days – you're the sweetest, gentlest man – *ille, nijamma* [no, really], look at me, Ramesh, look at me. Do I look like I think that way about you? Look at me. He's all warped now. He doesn't know what he's doing.

RAMESH. You never introduced me to your daughter.

MALINI. But you're not the reason for that, she is. I think you are a dear, darling man. (*Realises the door's locked.*) Open the door, Sharan. He's a gentle soul. He won't harm her. (*Pause.*) Deepa. Open the door! There's a limit to everything. I can't keep toiling for you forever.

Silence.

Sharan, don't be an idiot. *Kadhavuh tharaa!* [Open the door!]

Silence.

Tomorrow the crowd will be waiting for us. The whole world will be waiting in their living rooms with popcorn to see that. One of us or two of us, or all of us could get hurt tomorrow. All those people with bloodshot eyes and rough dirty hands. What will they do to her? Have you ever thought about that? Open the door!

49

RAMESH. Your children are constantly thinking dirty things. They're not normal.

MALINI. Forgive them, please.

RAMESH. How can I? He makes such an accusation . . . I only wanted to help you.

MALINI. I know, I know.

RAMESH. I . . . I think I should go now.

MALINI. No! They'll come out. Please, Ramesh, he didn't mean it at all. He's just a boy. It's the stress of the whole thing.

Silence.

RAMESH. He knows what he's saying. (*Pause.*) You need to speak to your children. I cannot take home an unwilling girl.

MALINI. Deepa, will you open the door? If you want to do one good thing in your life, then come out.

Silence.

Don't gang up against me. You'll regret this for the rest of your life.

Silence.

Deepa. *Velle vaa!* [Come out!] We'll all be safe. Don't listen to Sharan.

Silence.

I have to do something to salvage our life. Help me, Deepa. Please.

Silence.

RAMESH. I can come back later.

MALINI. No. Wait. They'll come out now. They have to.

Silence.

RAMESH. Malini, I . . . I'm sorry.

RAMESH *leaves.*

Scene Nine

Tuesday. 6 pm. SHARAN, MALINI *and* USHA. *Temple bell rings.*
USHA *is setting up the room for an interview.*

MALINI. Is this how the boards are for you?

> SHARAN *nods.*
>
> *Silence.*

Is she . . . ?

Silence.

SHARAN. I, I . . . I don't cross my legs when I write my exam. I sort
of go around my chair once before I sit on it.

MALINI. Why?

SHARAN. It's my lucky routine.

> *Silence.*
>
> We don't have to do this. Let's give the money back. And the
> bottles.
>
> *Silence.*
>
> I was wrong, okay? We can figure something else out.
>
> MALINI *shakes her head.*

USHA. Shh. Twenty seconds.

SHARAN. No. No. Ma, let's –

MALINI. Sharan, *chumma iru* [keep quiet].

USHA. Sit down.

> MALINI *hesitates. She goes around the chair and sits on it.*
> *Silence.*
>
> Good evening, India. Welcome to this very special episode of
> *Nation's Newsmakers*, the show with a difference. I'm Usha Singh
> and I'm travelling South of the Vindhyas today. For many years,
> Chennai was seen as a deeply conservative city, steeped in years of
> tradition, superstition and patriarchy. It was known as much for its
> stringent value system as for its music and dance. But recent

51

developments have eroded that perception. There is more to the city than we thought. Chennai appears to be as avant-garde as any other Indian metro and its youngsters sexually forward in a way the rest of India couldn't have imagined. Yes, indeed, I have with me, Malini Haridas, mother of the famous, or infamous, MMS girl. First of all, Malini, let me begin by asking you what you felt, as a mother, when you learnt what your daughter had done. (*Pause.*) Malini? (*Pause.*) Malini, can you tell us, what went through your mind when you discovered your daughter's act?

MALINI *reads from a paper.*

MALINI. I was shocked and –

USHA. You have to be louder.

MALINI (*reads without looking into the camera*). I was shocked and agonised –

USHA. Look into the camera.

MALINI (*without looking into the camera*). I was shocked and agonised by what my daughter had done out of foolishness and love. What she did was unacceptable and shameful, and she regrets her impulsive act. I, on her behalf as well as my own, humbly beg the forgiveness of her school, the residents of Shakti Complex, the people of Chennai, and my fellow (*Clears her throat.*) fellow countrymen for causing pain, suffering and disgrace. I humbly . . . (*Clears throat.*) I humbly request all the people who have gathered at my gates to rest assured that we are proud to be Tamils. I have tried to teach my children the importance of Tamil values and of staying within the bounds of the society we live in. I, as her mother, take full responsibility for my failure to ensure that my daughter understood the consequences of transgression. I request all the people to kindly disperse and allow the normal passage of life. The residents of Shakti Complex should not have to suffer for the indiscretion of my daughter. Thank you for your patience and time.

Pause.

USHA. Back to Vinay at the studio. When we return, more on the MMS issue. (*Pause.*) Don't move, Sharan – the wires!

SHARAN. No more.

USHA. Remember the deal. It's all or nothing. If you walk out now . . . You've already come this far. Let's finish it.

SHARAN. Enough, Ma. Let's stop it at this.

MALINI. Sharan. *Po. Po, da*. [Go.]

He hesitates. Finally he moves away.

USHA. Ten seconds.

MALINI *nods. Pause.* MALINI *tries to control her emotions.*

Welcome back to this very special episode of *Nation's News-makers* and I'm Usha Singh. Our question for you viewers is: Who do you think should be held responsible for the MMS incident? A) Parents, B) the school, or C) the society. SMS your answers to the number flashing on your screens right now because one of you will win a trip for two to Tokyo. And now, to the highlight of the evening. We have with us a very special guest. She's very young, only fifteen years old, but already she's stirred the imagination of an entire nation. Is she a femme fatale or is she the next icon of feminism? Or is she simply the girl next door? Who is she? And why did she do what she did? Let's find out. Please welcome, Deepa Haridas, India's most-watched teenager . . .

A Nick Hern Book

Free Outgoing first published in Great Britain in 2007 as a paperback original by Nick Hern Books Limited, 14 Larden Road, London W3 7ST, in association with the Royal Court Theatre, London

Cover image: Carole Verbyst
Cover design: Ned Hoste, 2H

Typeset by Nick Hern Books, London
Printed in the UK by CPI Bookmarque, Croydon, CR0 4TD

A CIP catalogue record for this book is available from the British Library

ISBN 978 1 85459 570 6